THE INDIAN SCIENCE OF ASTROLOGY

A GUIDE TO THE HISTORY AND PRACTICE OF JYOTISHA

DR. JAGADEESH PILLAI

Made with ♥ on the Notion Press Platform
www.notionpress.com

|| Dedicated to all wisdom seekers around the world ||

Contents

Contents

Prayer

**"Om Bhadram Karnebhih Shrunuyaama
DevaahBhadram Pashyemaakshabhiryajatraah
SthirairangaistushtuvaamsastanoobhihVyashema
Devahitam YadaayuhSwasti Na Indro
VridhashravaahSwasti Nah Pooshaa
VishwavedaahSwasti Nastaarkshyo ArishtanemihSwasti
No Brihaspatir DadhaatuOm Shantih, Shantih, Shantih"**

The literal meaning of this mantra is: OM. O Gods! Let us hear auspicious words from our ears. O reverent Gods! Let us behold propitious visions from our eyes, let our organs and body be stable, healthy, and strong. Let us do that which is pleasing to the gods in the life span allotted to us. May Indra, inscribed in the scriptures, bring us fortune! May Pushan, the knower of the world, grant us prosperity! May Trakshya, who vanquishes enemies, bestow us with blessings! May Brihaspati bring us success!
OM Peace, Peace, Peace.

About The Author

Dr. Jagadeesh Pillai is a renowned Guinness World Record holder, writer, and researcher hailing from Varanasi, also known as the abode of Lord Shiva. With a Ph.D. in Vedic Science and a range of creative ideas and achievements, he is a true polymath. He is the author of more than 100 books including Research Publications. Although his roots can be traced back to Kerala, the people of Varanasi hold him in high regard and affectionately consider him one of their own.

Dr. Pillai has achieved four Guinness World Records in the following subjects:

"Script to Screen" - In this record, Dr. Pillai produced and directed an animation film within the shortest time possible, breaking the previous record set by Canadians. He has also received numerous national and international awards and recognitions for this achievement.

Longest Line of Postcards - For this record, Dr. Pillai created a line of 16,300 postcards on the occasion of the 163rd anniversary of Indian Postal Day. The event also included a questionnaire about the Indian flag.

Largest Poster Awareness Campaign - Dr. Pillai designed an awareness campaign on the subject of "Beti Bachao - Beti Padhao" (Save the Girl Child - Educate the Girl Child) to achieve this record.

Largest Envelope - In tribute to the Indian Prime Minister's

"Make in India" initiative, Dr. Pillai created a 4000 square meter envelope using waste paper to achieve this record.

Attempted - **70000 Candles on a 210 kg Cake** - To celebrate the 70th Indian Independence Day, Dr. Pillai attempted to light 70,000 candles on a 210 kg cake, which was recorded in World Records India.

Attempted - **Documentary on Dhamek Stupa of Sarnath in 17 Languages** - Dr. Pillai attempted to create a documentary on the Dhamek Stupa of Sarnath, dubbing it in 17 different languages. The result of this attempt is currently awaiting confirmation from the Guinness World Records.

Dr. Pillai is skilled in teaching the Bhagavad Gita, a Hindu scripture, and is popular among young people. He has helped many young people improve their lives through his motivational teachings.

In addition to teaching, he has composed and sung numerous Sanskrit Bhajans and patriotic songs.

He has also written and directed several short films and documentaries for awareness campaigns, and has volunteered with the police in both UP and Kerala to spread awareness about various issues through videos and photography.

Incredibly, he has produced and directed over 100 documentaries about the city of Varanasi, all on his own.

He has also helped and guided more than 25 boys and girls to achieve world records through creative and innovative methods. He is a multifaceted person who uses his intellect and the blessings given to him by God to excel in various areas. He is both a teacher and a student, always learning and teaching, and is able to master any subject he comes across.

He is a selfless social activist and motivational speaker who has overcome struggles and failures to become a successful and enthusiastic individual with a rich life experience.

In addition to his work with the Bhagavad Gita, he is also an efficient Tarot card reader, Astro-Vastu consultant, and a talented singer and composer. He has sung the entire Ram Charita Manas and Bhagavad Gita in his own compositions, and has sung the phrase "Lokah Samastha Sukhino Bhavantu" in 50 different languages. He is currently working on a detailed and scientific study of Vedas, Upanishads, Puranas, and the Bhagavad Gita. He has also composed and sung the Hanuman Chalisa and Gayatri Mantra in 108 and 1008 different compositions, respectively.

Awards - Four Times Guinness World Records, Winner of Mahatma Gandhi Vishwa Shanti Puraskar, Mahatma Gandhi Global Peace Ambassador, Kashi Ratna Award, Dr. APJ Abdul Kalam Motivational Person of the Year 2017, Mother Teresa Award, Indira Gandhi Priyadarshini Award, Bharat Vikas Ratna Award, Udyog Ratna Award, Vigyan Prasar Award, Poorvanchal Ratn Samman.

Preface

The ancient practice of astrology has been in existence for many centuries, and it has a long history of being used as a tool for forecasting and understanding the future. Before the advent of modern science and technology, astrologers used to look at the stars, planets, and other celestial bodies to discover hidden meaning and make predictions. The science of astrology, known as Jyotisha, seeks to explain and understand the relationship between physical and spiritual events.

Jyotisha is based on the belief that the position of the planets in the heavens has a profound influence on life on earth. According to this belief, the planets are like messengers of the gods, who can give clues as to our actions in this world and the destiny that awaits us in the afterlife. By studying and understanding the placement of celestial bodies, astrologers gain insight into our future prospects, both good and bad.

In the Jyotish tradition, the planets are divided into nine classes, according to their position in the sky. These nine classes are related to various aspects of life, such as wealth, health, love, and career. Astrologers study these planets in order to assess a person's individual strengths and weaknesses, as well as their overall prospects for success in the future.

When consulting a Jyotish astrologer, one must consider various factors, such as their birth chart, the transits of the planets, and the current planetary cycles in order to make accurate predictions. They also consult published ephemerides, or astronomical tables that show the positions of the planets on any given date. By reading and interpreting the planetary alignment, astrologers are able to provide detailed readings regarding one's future prospects.

In addition to the science of astrology, Jyotish astrologers also offer a variety of traditional practices that are used to help clients achieve balance, insight, and inner peace. Some of these involve meditation, yoga, and the use of mantras. By practicing these methods, clients can gain access to higher levels of spiritual understanding.

Thus, when one considers the scope of Jyotish, it is clear that it is founded upon the belief that all events are interconnected, and that there is a cosmic order to all things. Along with the scientific and spiritual aspects of astrology, Jyotish also promotes the study of history and ancient texts so that one can more effectively understand how their present decisions will affect their future path.

I

Introduction: The Origins of Jyotisha

The origin of Jyotisha, or the Indian science of astrology, is believed to date back to the Vedic Age in ancient India, around 3000 BCE. It is thought to have been developed as a method to better understand and predict the cycle of planetary influences and their effects on nature and human life. Over the centuries, Jyotisha has evolved and is still practiced extensively all over the world today. It is based on the belief that the positions of the planets and other celestial bodies at the time of a person's birth can influence their life and fate. Along with its more spiritual aspects, Jyotisha also includes mathematical calculations related to the planets, stars, and other heavenly bodies. In addition to being practiced for centuries in India, Jyotisha has also been adopted in other parts of the world. In its modern form, Jyotisha has been used for everything from relationship counseling to predicting future events. In its most traditional form, Jyotisha is used to determine an individual's destiny and to make important life decisions. Despite its long history, Jyotisha is still widely practiced today and continues to be an important part of Hindu culture.

The term Jyotisha derives from 'jyoti' meaning 'light or ray' thereby implying the knowledge of light, as well as its relationship to the stars in the night sky and other celestial bodies. Jyotisha is based largely on astronomical observations of the movements and positions of these stars, planets and other celestial bodies in the night sky, thus helping to predict and explain key events like eclipses, weather, climate and other natural phenomena on the earth.

In its most basic form, the Vedic system of Jyotisha is divided into two main branches, Samhita and Sidhanta. Samhita deals with the planet-to-planet interactions, including their distances from one another and their impacts on the earth, while Sidhanta deals with calculations to predict the precise times of various relevant astronomical events, such as the beginning and end of an eclipse, or the alignment of two planets in particular configurations.

In addition to its astronomical uses, the Vedic system of Jyotisha is also applied to mundane matters and destiny forecasting in order to offer advice and guidance to its followers. It works by using precise mathematical calculations based on an individual's date, time and place of birth to create a personalized chart known as a kundali. This is then used as a basis to interpret an individual's present life circumstances and give an indication of what the future may hold.

Jyotisha is a complex art and science that requires the study of multiple aspects. It offers both the general knowledge of cosmic events, and personalized insights for those looking for orientations and guidance in life. This age-old science finds application in several aspects of modern-day life including in ritualistic and religious practices, astrological counseling, health and wellbeing, education and career guidelines, wealth and finance, relationships and marriage, etc. As such, many people across the world find solace in the knowledge of Jyotisha and its precision in predicting the future.

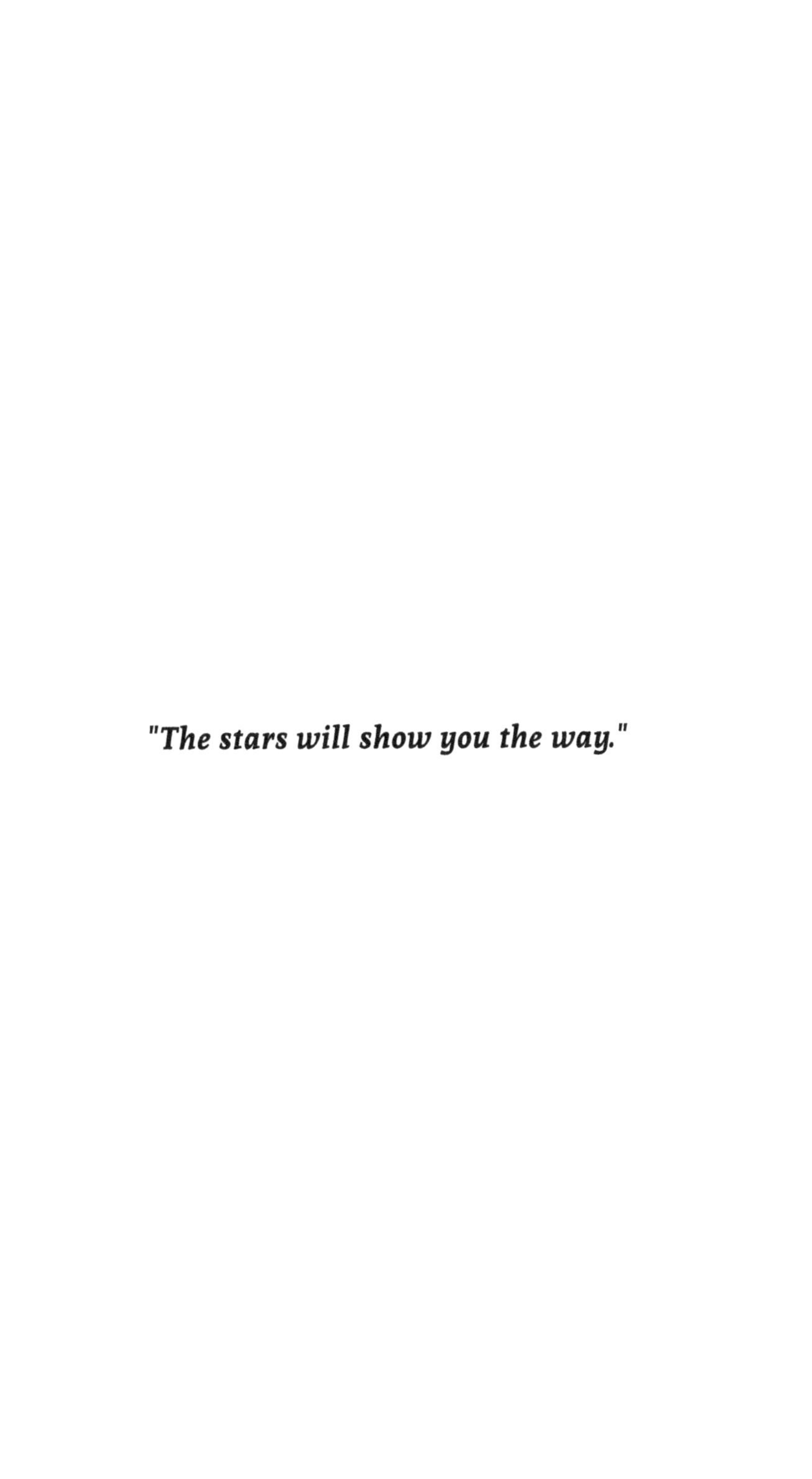
"The stars will show you the way."

II

The Development of Jyotisha in Vedic Literature

Jyotisha, or astrology, is a form of knowledge that emerged in ancient Vedic literature. Vedic astrology has evolved greatly over the centuries, developing a complex and intricate system of divinatory practices and rituals.Jyotisha refers to the "science of light," and its origin is rooted in the need to protect and promote human welfare. This ancient practice is related to the Vedic concept of the universe and is used to explore the relationship between a person's life and the stars and planets.

In the Vedic literature, Jyotisha is connected to samhitas, or the recitation of mantras for the god's and personal purposes. Jyotisha is also related to Vedic texts associated with ritual practices and astronomy. These practices include mantra, priestly ceremonies, and seasonal observances. The texts contain references to planets, asterisms, numerology, astrology, constellations, and other divine entities.

In the earliest Vedic literature, Jyotisha was used primarily for divination and predictive purposes. This includes predicting the future and/or foretelling events. This type of astrology included the use of mantras and prayers to gain cosmic knowledge related to practical aspects of life such as marriage, children, career, and health.

As time passed, the practice of Jyotisha began to expand. It developed to include the study of the stars and planets, calculating their positions in the firmament, and interpreting their influence on the lives of humans. In the Upanishads, Jyotisha was given a spiritual component, and its practitioners were considered Brahmins. Later, the concepts of astronomy, astrology, and astrology-medicine were combined, called Jyotisha shastra orastrology-medicine.

Finally, during the medieval period, the practice of Jyotisha became increasingly more complex, with more sophisticated and intricate observations, predictions, and computations. In this era, the Vedas became more extensively studied, and their concepts were used in the practice of Jyotisha. These concepts included the use of horoscopes and the calculation of planetary influences.

The development of Jyotisha in Vedic literature reflects the importance that life events have had in the Vedic tradition. Jyotisha is connected to Vedic rituals which involve not only knowledge about the cosmos and its influences on life, but also the respect and reverence for higher powers. While Jyotisha is an ancient practice, it is still an important part of modern Hinduism and has been adapted and changed to keep up with the changing times.

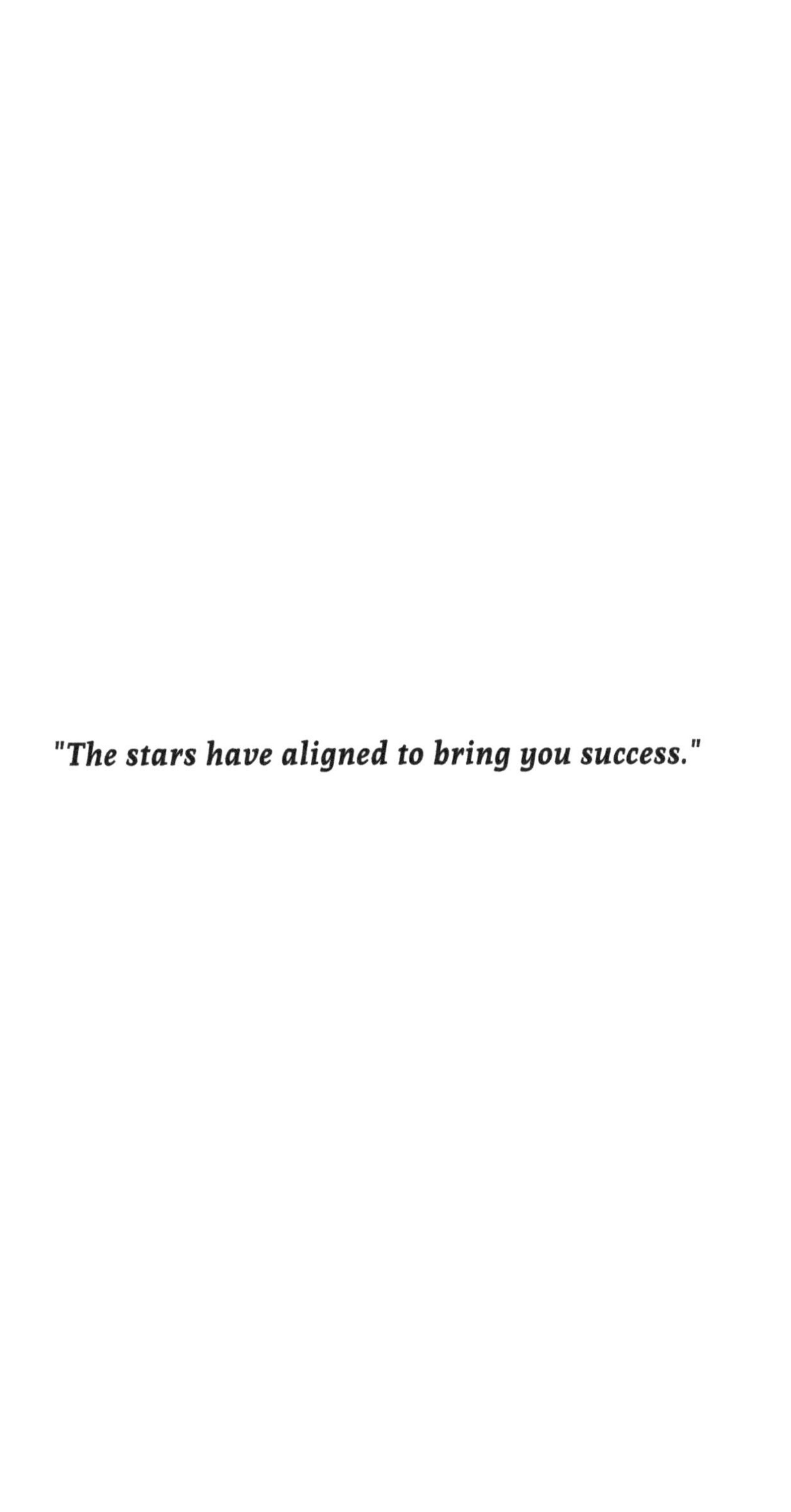

"The stars have aligned to bring you success."

III

The Classical Period of Jyotisha: The Astrological treatises

The classical period of Jyotisha, or Vedic astrology, was a period of great development in the Indian astrological tradition which dates back to at least the sixth century B.C. In this period, a number of important astrological treatises were composed which laid the foundations for the practice of Jyotisha even today.

The root of the Indian astrological tradition is the Vedas, the ancient texts which are among the oldest and most important of Hindu scriptures. The Vedas contain a significant amount of information on astrology, including elements of predictive astrology, as well as instructions on how to perform rituals related to astronomy. The earliest

Vedic astrological treatises likely date back to the sixth century B.C., and by the fourth century B.C., astrology had become well-established with a distinct set of teachings, rituals, and practices.

The classical period of Jyotisha was a time of great development in the astrological tradition. During this period, a number of seminal works were composed, including the Brihat Parashara Hora Shastra and the Varga Varga Sanhita. These text laid the foundations for modern astrological practice, introducing the 12 zodiac signs, planetary combinations and the significations associated with them, as well as the meaning of Vedic celestial bodies. These texts also laid out the basis for predicting the future, and outlined numerous divination techniques.

The classical period of Jyotisha also saw the emergence of two important mathematical branches which were essential for astrological calculations. These were jyotishya and ganit, which are two forms of Indian mathematical theory. This enabled astrologers to make more accurate calculations, such as predicting eclipses and other planetary movements.

The classical period is also remembered for its great astrologers, who left behind some important treatises. Among the most important are Varah Mimamsa by Kalyana Varma and Phala Deepika by Mantresa Misra. These texts laid down the foundations of modern Indian astrology, which still follows many of their teachings today.

The classical period was a period of great development in the Indian astrological tradition. During this period, the foundations of modern astrology were laid down in a number of important treatises. This period also saw the emergence of important mathematical branches which made astrological calculations more accurate. Finally, great astrologers of this period left behind some important treatises that still form the basis of modern Indian astrology.

"Anyone can be a millionaire, but to become a billionaire one needs an astrologer"

ജ

IV

The Techniques of Jyotisha: Reading a Horoscope

Jyotisha, also known as "Vedic astrology," is an ancient system of understanding the movements of the Sun, Moon and other planets, and the effects they have on our lives. It is believed to have originated over 6,000 years ago and has been subject to further study and refinement since that time. Jyotisha is the science of forecasting the future and predicting events based on the positions of the planets and stars. Reading a horoscope is a key part of Jyotisha, and involves analyzing charts of the sky to gain insight into a person's life and destiny.

The chart used in Jyotisha is called a "Rashi chart," and it is created with the assistance of a software program. The Rashi chart will contain all of the major planets, such as the Sun, Moon, mercury, Mars, Venus, and Jupiter. Each of these planets will be located in one of the 12 houses of the sky – Aries, Taurus, Gemini, Cancer, Leo, Virgo, Libra, Scorpio, Sagittarius, Capricorn, Aquarius, or Pisces. These are referred to as the "astrological houses." The position of each planet in each house will be different for every individual, and this is what makes each person's horoscope unique.

In order to read a person's horoscope, a Jyotish practitioner will first study the Rashi chart. They will then assess the planets in relation to the houses, and look for patterns and influence. For example, the Sun will indicate a person's overall health and focus in life, while the Moon will show emotional and domestic matters. While these interpretations are set according to tradition, they can be modified to fit the individual.

Wall charts and mathematical equations are also used extensively in Jyotisha. The placement of the planets within the 12 houses is based on mathematics, and these equations are used to determine when certain aspects of the chart come into play. This can include determining when one planet is in a stronger or weaker position than another, or when certain planets are in certain houses.

Jyotisha also uses doshas, which are combinations of the planets and their positions, to provide insight into a person's fate. Doshas are divided into "functional," or positive aspects, and "deficient" or negative aspects. By studying the doshas, a Jyotish practitioner can provide advice on how to move forward in life and fulfill one's destiny.

As you can see, reading a horoscope is a complex but meaningful process. With the help of a skilled and experienced Jyotish practitioner, an individual can gain insight into their life, their destiny, and how best to move forward for the greatest success in life and career.

"The stars will light your path."

V

The Jyotisha system of prediction

The Jyotisha system, also known as Indian or Vedic astrology, is an ancient system of divination from India. It is based on planetary placements and dates of birth that can be used to draw conclusions about a person's past, present, and future fortune. The accuracy of Jyotisha can depend on the skill of the astrologer, as well as the quality of the software used to generate an accurate representation of the sky.

The basic principles of Jyotisha, as with many other forms of astrology, come from tracking the movement of the sun, moon, and planets across the sky and associating them with particular elements, qualities, and energies. For example, the sun is often associated with stability and leadership, while the moon is considered to be related to emotion and intuition. Depending on the position of these celestial bodies relative to each other, different interpretations can be made about the future.

In addition to the traditional Jyotisha system, which requires the use of a trained astrologer, modern technology has allowed predictive software programs to be used to create accurate predictions. These software programs are able to generate detailed astrological maps of the sky from a specified moment in time. The accuracy of the map and its predictions depend on the complexity and accuracy of the software. If the software is sufficiently accurate, it can often be used to create predictions about a given individual's future.

Though accurate predictions require an astrologer to correctly interpret the map provided by the software, the accuracy of astrological predictions can vary greatly depending on the experience and skill of the astrologer. Thus, predictions made from a well-trained astrologer who has access to sophisticated software and detailed charts can often offer reliable and accurate predictions.

The Jyotisha system of predictions is an ancient and highly developed system of divination. With access to the right software and an experienced astrologer, the accuracy of Jyotisha predictions can be quite reliable. For those who are interested in exploring this system of prediction, it's important to seek out experienced and skilled astrologers to ensure the accuracy of the results.

"Trust in the power of astrology to unlock your potential."

VI

The use of Jyotisha in daily life

Jyotisha, also known as Indian Astrology, is the ancient practice of analyzing the positions of the stars, planets, and other celestial bodies in order to predict future events, gain insight into a person's character, and bring harmony and balance into their life. It is one of the oldest and most widely practiced forms of astrology in the world, and millions of Hindus, Buddhists, and Jains use it in their daily lives.

Jyotisha has been used for centuries to assess relationships and recognize the potential for a successful marriage union. The nine planets, along with the stars, have been categorized into 27 nakshatras or constellations, each of which has a specific influence on the compatibility between two individuals. By examining how the nakshatras and planets interact, Jyotishis (traditional astrologers) can study the karmic connections between two individuals and make predictions as to the likely outcome of a proposed marriage.

Jyotisha can also be used to provide insight into a person's career path. Through analysis of the nakshatras and planets, Jyotishis can identify opportunities for advancement and tell when a person's career is likely to peak or dip. This information can be incredibly useful for individuals who are trying to make informed decisions about their future career paths.

Jyotisha can also be used to provide advice on the best times to embark on new ventures and activities. Certain constellations are associated with different kinds of activities, and by studying the positions of the stars and planets, it is possible to determine which constellations are best suited to a particular venture. This information can be used to inform decisions regarding when to start a new business, launch a product, or enter a new market.

In addition to providing invaluable advice on relationships, careers, and timing, Jyotisha is also used to provide guidance on the decisions we make in our everyday lives. By examining the nakshatras and planets, Jyotishis can determine the most fortuitous course of action for any given situation. This can be an invaluable asset in helping us make decisions that are in line with our true destiny and bring joy and harmony into our lives.

Jyotisha is an ancient science that is used by millions of people to gain insight into their lives, relationships, and destinies. By studying the nakshatras and planets, Jyotishis can help people make informed decisions regarding their careers and relationships, as well as provide advice on the best times to embark on new projects and activities. In this way, Jyotisha is a powerful and invaluable tool in helping us make decisions that bring harmony and balance into our daily lives.

"Your fate lies in the hands of the gods above."

VII

The Influence of Jyotisha on Indian Culture & Society

Jyotisha is a branch of Vedic astrology originating in India, which has been used for centuries to study the movements of stars and planets to provide far-reaching insights into areas such as astrology, astronomy, geography, mathematics, timekeeping and law. In modern times, Jyotisha is used to guide future decisions, health and well-being, to improve relationships and to explore spiritual growth. For thousands of years, Jyotisha has been an integral part of Indian culture and society.

In India, Jyotisha is believed to be the "eye of destiny", strongly influencing the attitudes and decisions of individuals. It is known as Vedanga, one of the six Vedic sciences, and it is used as a guide to make important life decisions, manage relationships, choose a business or marry. To this end, Jyotishis (astrologers) rely heavily on the knowledge of predictive principles derived from the stars, planets and other astronomical objects to gain insight into a person's life. In addition to making predictions for individuals, Jyotishis often provide solutions to problems based on their astrological insights.

Jyotisha has also had a strong influence on the day-to-day lives of Indian people and in the way the social order changes. For example, Indian festivals and holidays are often timed according to Jyotisha, ensuring they occur when the stars and planets are properly aligned. The dates of important ceremonies, events and rituals also often depend on Jyotisha readings. The influence of Jyotisha extends beyond India - it is used to time foreign business decisions, wedding dates and engage wealthy Indian families with up-to-date astrological predictions.

The influence of Jyotisha on Indian culture is immense and can be seen in the way Indians negotiate their relationships, the decisions they make on important events and the way they plan their future. It is an integral part of the Indian worldview and pervades ancient, complex Indian civilizations. The reliance on astrological readings to predict the future and make decisions is something that is deeply engrained in the Indian psyche. Consequently, Jyotisha has become an important factor in how modern Indian people make decisions and plan their lives - from what career to pursue, to who to marry or how best to look after one's health.

Jyotisha has been an integral part of Indian culture for thousands of years and it continues to be used to guide important decisions and rituals today. Its influence extends beyond the borders of India, with many wealthy families seeking the counsel of Jyotishis to aid in planning their future. With its hints at destiny and powerful predictive abilities, Jyotisha continues to be a major source of information and guidance in Indian culture and society.

"Let astrology be your guide through life's journey."

VIII

Jyotisha & Ayurveda: The Intersection of Astrology & Medicine

The ancient Indian sciences of Jyotisha and Ayurveda have been interconnected for centuries as two related branches of knowledge that share key philosophical foundations. Jyotisha is an ancient system of astrology that works with how planetary movements relate to the rhythms of nature and individual human lives. Ayurveda is an ancient science of life, healing and preventative medicine with a comprehensive view of health and wellbeing. As separate systems, Jyotisha and Ayurveda each have distinct purposes, yet share common convictions regarding the integral relationship between the cosmic forces beyond our control and the body-mind systems under our influence.

Jyotisha, which literally translates to "the science of light", is the study of astronomical bodies and their positions in relation to the fate of individuals and societies throughout the world. Ancient Jyotisha texts instruct how the timing of events can be established based on individual birth charts – which take into consideration the zodiac midnight positions of planets, the movement of the planets and the nodes – as well as the dasha system, which outlines the hierarchical influences of theses planets throughout a lifetime. Their influences can be seen in family life, daily routine chores, optimum career paths, and spiritual development.

Ayurveda, which translates to "the science of life", works on the principle that the human body should be understood as part of nature and should therefore be treated holistically. It is the oldest known science of life, balancing the energies in the body (Vata, Pitta, and Kapha) through dietary and lifestyle advice suited to the individual constitution. This is described in ancient Ayurvedic texts such as Charaka Samhita, Sushruta Samhita, and Vagbhata Samhita as well as the primary Vedic texts. Ayurveda works to restore balance by addressing stressors and disharmonies, through specific interventions tailored to the individual needs of the client.

Where Jyotisha and Ayurveda meet is in their shared understandings about the interconnectedness of all life forms, the cyclical patterns in nature, and the power of language, symbols and rituals. Both fields work from the acknowledgement that physical health on the Earth is directly related to the patterns of the macrocosmos. For example, the position of the planets at the time of birth can indicate potential physical, mental and emotional challenges, and practitioners can thereby make connections between individual birth charts and related Ayurvedic points for health maintenance.

Collectively, Jyotisha and Ayurveda create a powerful system of knowledge which acknowledges the effects which planetary movements and cosmic forces have on an individual's health, destiny and samskaras (past impressions). These understandings, combined with the use of various rituals and healing therapies, ensures the growth and wellbeing of the individual and encourages them to come into harmony.

"Astrology can help you find balance and harmony in life."

IX

The Modern Study and Practice of Jyotisha

The modern study and practice of Jyotisha, often referred to as Vedic Astrology, is an insightful and multi-faceted subject. Jyotisha is an ancient science passed down through generations of Vedic scholars, resulting in a complex and fascinating discipline.

Jyotisha encompasses a wide array of beliefs, symbols and concepts. The fundamentals of the study include an understanding of the planets and their influences, the positions of the stars, and the nature of the cosmos. By examining these components, Jyotisha is able to provide insight into the connections between a person's life path, their fortune and their potential destiny.

In the modern era, Jyotisha is blended with updated

science, technology and cultural influences, giving it a broad range of interpretations. Modern practitioners are practiced in a wide range of analytical methods, including both Western and Eastern forms.

One of the most common methods used in modern Jyotisha is Predictive Astrology, which involves an in-depth analysis of an individual's birth chart. By reading the various signs, symbols and information within the birth chart, practitioners are able to accurately detect patterns and influences in that person's life. This type of analysis is often combined with a more philosophical approach to astrology, focusing on the ways in which the planetary energies are connected to the person's value system, core traits and destiny.

In addition to analysis, modern Jyotisha includes a wide range of spiritual practices, such as chanting mantras, meditating, and connecting with Divine energies through rituals. By understanding the cycles of the planets and moon, Jyotisha can also be used to determine optimum times for certain events or tasks.

Overall, Jyotisha is an ancient and powerful practice, adapted to fit the needs of modern life. By studying the various signs, symbols and influences of the planets and stars, astrologers are able to gain insight into a person's life path, and guide them towards a more prosperous future. Whether it's for personal enlightenment, spiritual guidance, or practical decision-making, Jyotisha provides an incredibly diverse and effective tool for understanding the complexity of the cosmos.

"Astrology can help you make sense of life's complexities."

X

Criticism and Controversies Surrounding Jyotisha

In the East, a renowned form of divination known as Jyotisha, or Vedic (Hindu) astrology, practices the art of interpreting the position of celestial objects in order to determine their influence on both personal and global events. It has been employed for centuries, yet the practice is not without its share of controversy and criticism.

When it comes to critics of Jyotisha, it is easy to see why many people find its concepts flawed. For one, astrologers make predictions with little to no evidence or scientific proof to support their claims. Furthermore, when it comes to making predictions about future events, astrologers rely heavily upon assumptions and subjective judgement. This does not sit well with the more scientifically-minded among us, since the lack of empiricism can be seen as unsound. These factors have caused some to dismiss the entire field as an unreliable source of knowledge.

In addition, many argue that Jyotisha is simply used as a way of exploiting those who are vulnerable. This is especially true of those who are suffering from depression or mental illness and may be more willing to seek out advice from astrologers. It can be disheartening to find out that these people are often taken advantage of without being fully aware of what they are getting into.

What is more, some people are concerned about the implications of Jyotisha for religious beliefs. In particular, some people argue that astrology can lead to a reliance on superstition or a reliance on gods and goddesses to guide one's life. This can create a lazy attitude and prevent people from actively engaging with their own choices and decisions.

On the other hand, there are those who believe that such criticism is misguided and overlooks the importance of Jyotisha in the larger context of traditional Hinduism and its beliefs. These people argue that astrological readings can provide meaningful insight into life's complex problems and can serve to complement the search for understanding of self. They also point out that many astrologers who practice ethically offer valuable advice in regards to personal and professional decisions.

No matter who has the right perspective on the debate, it is clear that there are rigid criticisms and controversies surrounding Jyotisha. Due to the lack of scientific evidence, some deny the legitimacy of the entire field. Others are concerned about the exploitation of vulnerable people and the implication it has for religious beliefs. Meanwhile, those who champion the practice emphasize its ability to act as a useful complement to personal decision making and its rightful place in traditional Hindu belief.

"Astrology can provide insight into yourself and others around you."

XI

Western Astrology and its relation to Jyotisha

Western Astrology and its relation to Jyotisha (astrology) have both been used for centuries as spiritual techniques to gain insight into an individual's life. While Western Astrology is a popular system within well-developed nations, it can be traced back to Aristotle's On the Heavens for its foundations. This astrological system is considered a predictive occult art, meaning it is based on a person's birth chart and the corresponding positions of the planets in the houses of the zodiac in order to draw predictions about possible events and life paths. Western astrology can be divided into three categories: Hellenistic, Medieval and Modern. Hellenistic astrology is an ancient form of astrology born by combining Babylonian astrology and Greek philosophy, while Medieval astrology is an evolution of the Hellenistic system and also incorporates forms of

Hindu astrology called Jyotish. Modern Western astrology developed out of the Medieval astrological literature after the Italian Renaissance.

Jyotisha, or Indian astrology, is a Vedic practice, or form of Hindu astrology, that is based on the movements of the sun and moon, as well as other cosmic phenomena and activities. Jyotish emphasizes the influence of karma and the comparison of the personality of the individual with the functions of the different planets in the solar system. Jyotish shares many aspects with Western astrology, such as its symbols, signs, and concepts of time; however, it also contains unique components, such as Hindu deities and Vedic mantras, making it more spiritually rooted and focused on connecting life to the divine. Utilizing the knowledge of Jyotish, a practitioner of the art is able to advise the individual they are working with on how to maximize their success in any area of life and spiritual growth.

Both Western astrology and Jyotish are powerful tools for personal and spiritual development. Western Astrology can often give insight into a person's life path and purpose, and Jyotish focuses more on the spiritual nature and development of the individual. Both can be used to draw from a person's potential and inner resources, as well as providing advice and guidance on how to increase the individual's potential and progress in the most beneficial way possible. These systems offer light and clarity to those who choose to pursue it, and can lead to greater fulfillment, joy and harmony.

"India – a land where one need not bother with looking good, but rather embracing natural beauty"

XII

Jyotisha (astrology) in the digital age: Software & Online Services

Astrology, which dates back to the 3rd millennium BC, has long been considered a form of divination used to chart the movements of the planets and starsin order to better understand the influences they have on our lives. Astrology has experienced a resurgence in recent years, and the digital age has played a role in that revival. Software and online services have expanded the reach of astrology, allowing astrologers to reach clients all over the world.

Software designed for astrologers gives them the ability to quickly and accurately process complex planetary positions. Whereas before astrologers would have to manually compute the positions of celestial bodies, now powerful software programs do all the heavy lifting, freeing astrologers to focus on giving their clients meaningful interpretations. Some popular astrology software programs, such as Solar Fire, offer an array of powerful features, from detailed birth charts to customizable reports.

Online astrology services are also creating a new wave of opportunities for astrologers. A large number of websites now exist that allow astrologers to offer services online, such as personalized readings and consultations. These websites, such as Kepler and Ophiuchus, make astrological advice available to anyone who has an internet connection. They also provide a much easier way for astrologers to build their client base, as they are no longer limited to their geographic area. Now, they can easily connect with clients from all over the world, potentially making a lucrative living from their craft.

The digital age has given astrology an unprecedented thrust into the 21st century, paving the way for advancements and opportunities that were unthinkable before. The expansive product range of software and online services have revolutionized the field, and opened up a realm of possibilities for astrologers, as well as clients seeking answers to life's mysteries.

"You have a penetrating mind today with excellent concentration and focus"

ꟸ

XIII

Jyotisha (astrology) impact in Business and Career Guidance

Jyotisha (astrology) is an ancient science that has been practiced for thousands of years in India and other parts of the world. It is a form of prediction and guidance based on the movement and alignment of the stars and planets. One of the many uses of Jyotisha is to gain insight into business and career choices.

Business and career decisions can be highly complex and involve innumerable factors, ranging from personal aptitude and interests to market forces, which necessitate the use of Jyotisha for more accurate predictions. As the celestial bodies have a direct influence on the fate of humans, consulting a qualified astrologer is an effective method of discerning prospects in the future.

Through Jyotisha, astrologers can assess the position of various astrological bodies in the individual's birth chart and make accurate predictions regarding the effects it will have on their career. They can provide guidance on which business choices are best suited for individual personalities and circumstances. Astrologers can also make predictions on periods when starting a business will be most successful according to their birth charts. This can help entrepreneurs determine when to launch their businesses, investment states, and when to expand. Astrologers can also advise on the potential success of diverse trades and even the types of businesses individuals should pursue in order to make the most of their potential and lead a financially secure life.

Jyotisha can also be used for predicting fluctuations in the stock market and commodities market. This can be useful for investors who wish to make decisions based on astrological insights. Furthermore, Jyotisha can be used to make predictions about competitive sectors for business and when to change jobs or careers.

In summary, Jyotisha plays a significant role in the business and career guidance of individuals. By paying attention to the various movements of the stars and planets, astrologers can provide individuals with accurate insight into their prospects in life. This can help them make well-informed decisions and become successful in their endeavors.

"A wise man should consider that health is the greatest of human blessings"

XIV

Jyotisha in Matchmaking and Relationship Compatibility

Jyotisha, or Vedic astrology, is a practice originating from ancient Indian and Eastern cultures. It has been used for hundreds of years to predict and interpret events, help with decision-making, and inform decisions about matchmaking and relationship compatibility.

Jyotisha begins with the belief that human beings are intrinsically linked to the universe and celestial bodies, and that by studying the ancient texts and planetary patterns one can gain wisdom, understanding and insight into the events, relationships and cycles of life. By studying an individual's birth chart, Jyotisha practitioners can gain insight into the compatibility and harmony of two individuals in a relationship.

Typically, Jyotisha focuses on the natal astrology or birth chart of an individual, which consists of nine planets in various Jupiter/Sun/Moon patterns. From this chart, practitioners look to interpret the individual's life and character, as well as make predictions about the future. Additionally, each planet is associated with different qualities, such as Mars being associated with ambition or Venus with love, which enable Jyotisha practitioners to interpret how two individuals might interact and how their relationship might develop.

The practice of matchmaking with Jyotisha involves looking at two individuals' natal charts in order to assess whether the two are compatible and harmonious with one another. This process involves looking at a variety of points, such as the Ascendant, planets and signs of each individual's chart and weighing how well these points interact.

Through a comparison of the signs and planets of an individual's birth chart to that of their potential partner, Jyotisha practitioners are able to assess the compatibility of a potential relationship. This process includes assessing both hemispheres of the chart, the interpersonal relationship aspects while also considering third party relationships outside the couple.

Jyotisha is an ancient practice used to interpret and prophesize events, inform decisions and assess relationship compatibility. Sinse Jyotisha is rooted in consulting the Vedic texts and the planetary patterns associated with a person's birth chart, it can provide insight into individual personalities and the potential for a harmonious relationship between two individuals.

"We owe a lot to Indians who taught us how to count without which no worthwhile scientific discovery could have been made"

XV

The ongoing relevance & significance of Jyotisha (Astrology)

Jyotisha, commonly known as Astrology, is an ancient practice and form of divination that has become increasingly popular in both India and the West over the centuries. Jyotisha, meaning "science of light" is the study of how celestial bodies influence and affect the lives, events, and destinies of all living things. Based on observations of the movements of planets and stars and the alignment of the planets around the Earth, Jyotisha is used to gain insight into potential problems, strengths, and opportunities present in the life of the individual.

At the core of Jyotisha is an understanding that the various celestial bodies have a direct connection to the lives of people. As these bodies travel through the universe, their energy and influence has an effect on events and on the lives of those people. By charting the progress of these bodies and the alignment in which they appear relative to the Earth, Jyotisha practitioners are able to gain insight into the various influences and perspectives of the planets on individuals and their lives. It is believed that this energy and influence can affect different points in time and the outcomes of certain events such as marriages and journeys, as well as everything in between.

In both traditional Hindu and Vedic culture as well as more modern Western astrology, Jyotisha is often used to make predictions and gain insight into personal relationships and matters of the heart. Vedic astrologers use a combination of astrological techniques and the use of the Hindu calendar and its lunar cycles to determine future events, often with great accuracy. In the West, astrological charts are often used to determine compatibility between two people and to analyse important relationship topics such as communication, commitment, and fidelity.

In more modern times, Jyotisha has become a popular tool for helping to make important life decisions such as career choices and financial investments in addition to helping individuals to gain insight into their love lives, health, and wellbeing. Even in this day and age when there are so many other options to help us make decisions and gain insight into our lives, Jyotisha is still an incredibly useful and popular way to gain insight into important matters.

It is clear to see that Jyotisha is still relevant and has a significant place in our lives. While its prevalence and influence on decision-making has certainly diminished in the modern world, it is still an incredibly valuable tool for helping to gain insight into important matters such as relationships, careers, and the future. Thanks to the popularity of astrology in both Hindu and Vedic culture, as well as among the general population, Jyotisha continues to be an important and ongoing part of many people's lives.

Other Books Of The Author

1. The Moments When I Met God
2. Kashiyile Theertha Pathangal
3. GURU GYAN VANI
4. Abhiprerak Gita
5. ASSI SE JAIN GHAT TAK
6. Hopelessness of Arjuna
7. The Soul and It's True Nature
8. Sense of Action (Karma)
9. Action through Wisdom
10. Action through Wisdom
11. THEORY AND PRACTICAL OF EVERY ACTION
12. LOGICAL UNDERSTANDING OF THE SUPREME
13. THE IMPERISHABLE SUPREME
14. Yatra Nishadraj se Hanuman Ghat Tak
15. Yatra Karnatak Ghat se Raja Ghat Tak
16. Yatra Pandey Ghat se Prayagraj Ghat Tak
17. Yatra Ranjendra Prasad Ghat se Dattatreya Ghat Tak
18. YaatraSindhiya Ghat se Gwaliar Ghat Tak
19. Yatra Mangala Gauri Ghat se Hanuman Gadhi Ghat Tak
20. Yatra Gaay Ghat Se Nishad Ghat Tak
21. MAA GANGA, GHATEN EVM UTSAV
22. Ganga Arti Dev Deepavali evam Any Utsav
23. Potentials of Digitalized India
24. VEDIC CONSCIOUSNESS
25. A Brief Introduction to Vedic Science
26. Kashi ke Barah Jyotirling
27. IMPACT OF MOTIVATION
28. Let's have a Milky Way Journey
29. Color Therapy in a Nutshell

30. Rigveda in a Nutshell
31. Yajurveda in a Nutshell
32. Samveda in a Nutshell
33. Atharva Veda in a Nutshell
34. Ayushman Bhava - Ayurveda
35. Srimad Bhagavad Gita and Upanishad Connection
36. Srimad Bhagavad Gita - an attempt to summarize each chapter.
37. Facts and Impact of Nakshatra
38. Astro Gems - NAVARATNA
39. Ekadashi - A Concise Overview
40. A Concise View of Hanuman Chalisa
41. Inspirational Gita
42. Nakshatraranyam
43. Summary of 18 Mahapuranas
44. Synopsis of 18 Upa Puranas
45. Rigvediya Upanishads
46. Shukla Yajurvediya Upanishads
47. Krishna Yajurvediya Upanishads
48. Samavediya Upanishads
49. Atharvavediya Upanishads
50. The Seven Great Sages
51. From Rocket Scientist to President Dr. APJ Abdul Kalam
52. The Visionary's Voice - Quotes of Dr. APJ Abdul Kalam
53. The Wisdom of Swami Vivekananda: Insights and Inspiration from a Legendary Spiritual Teacher
54. Ayurvedic Remedies from the Garden
55. Sages and Seers
56. Rising Strong – Motivational Stories of Women
57. Beyond Flames -Mystery stories of Funeral Ghat Manikarnika
58. The Origins of Tulsi: A Look at the Mythological Roots of the Plant"

59. The Holistic Cow: A Look at the Physical, Spiritual, and Cultural Importance of Cows in India
60. Arts of Healing
61. Exploring the Divine
62. Understanding Five Elements
63. The Etymology of Ram
64. Symbols of India
65. Voice of Change (About Speeches of Great Men)
66. She Speaks (About Speeches of Great Women)
67. Patriotism on Celluloid – Brief About Patriotic Films
68. The Music of Motivation: A Brief Guide to Inspirational Film Songs
69. **Unlocking the Secrets of the Dashopanishads**
70. A Cultural Mosaic
71. Ancient Traditions, Modern Minds
72. Ecos of Ancient Wisdom
73. Beneath the Surface
74. From Temples to Ashrams
75. Sages of the Subcontinent
76. The Art of Healling (Ayurveda, Yoga & Naturopathy)
77. Indian Kitchen
78. The Festivals of India
79. The Indian Epics Retold
80. The Power of Mantras
81. The Indian River Ganges
82. The Indian Architecture
83. Rites of Passage
84. The Indian Silk Road
85. The Indian Literature
86. The Indian Villages
87. The Indian Folks & Crafts
88. The Way of Buddha
89. The Ramayan of Tulsidas

90. Astrological Remedies
91. The Secret Power of Motivation
92. Secret of Developing your Inner Strength
93. The Secret Path to Motivation
94. The Art and Secret of Positive Thinking
95. The Secrets of Practicing Ethical Living
96. Indian Art and Painting
97. The Indian Herbalism
98. Bharatanatyam to Kathak
99. Exploring India's Astrological Remedies
100. The Indian Festival of Flowers
101. Indian Handicrafts
102. The Splashes of Joy – India's Colour Festival

CONTACT

DR. JAGADEESH PILLAI

PhD in Vedic Science

Four Times Guinness World Record Holder

Winner of Mahatma Gandhi Vishwa Shanti Puraskar and
Global Peace Ambassador

Gemology, Astro & Vastu Consultant - Spiritual Counselor

Consultant for designing World Record Ideas

Efficient Tarot Card Reader

9839093003

myrichindia@gmail.com

drjagadeeshpillai@facebook

drjagadeeshpillai@instagram

jagadeeshpillai@youtube

www. JAGADEESHPILLAI.com

ꝏ

|| LOKAHA SAMASTHAHA SUKHINO BHAVANTU ||

Printed by Libri Plureos GmbH in Hamburg,
Germany